WHEN YOU
FAST

THE WHY AND HOW OF
Christian Self-Discipline

L. Joseph Letendre

ANCIENT FAITH PUBLISHING

CHESTERTON, INDIANA

Published by:
    Ancient Faith Publishing
    A Division of Ancient Faith Ministries
    P.O. Box 748
    Chesterton, IN 46304

All Old Testament quotations, unless otherwise identified,
are from the Orthodox Study Bible, © 2008 by St. Athanasius
Academy of Orthodox Theology (published by Thomas Nelson,
Inc., Nashville, Tennessee) and are used by permission. New
Testament quotations are from the New King James Version
of the Bible, © 1982 by Thomas Nelson, Inc., and are used by
permission.

ISBN: 978-1-944967-97-0

LCCN: 2020952494

Printed in the United States of America

To my wife, Susan
With me always
in the striving, the sacrifices, and the joy:
Our Dance of Isaiah continues.

Contents

INTRODUCTION: Coming to Terms with Fasting   7

PART I: Why We Fast   13

1 Because of Christ and the Church   15

PART II: How We Fast   31

2 Fast with the Church   33

3 Choose Your Weapons   39

4 Avoid Extremes   45

5 Start with Food   51

6 Deny Yourself   59

7 Talk Less   65

8 Cultivate Silence   71

9 Exorcise Your Mind   79

10 Be Purposeful   87

APPENDIX: A Field Guide to Toxic Thoughts   91

About the Author   101

Coming to Terms with Fasting

mbedded in the middle of the Sermon on the Mount (Matt. 6) we find Jesus' instruction regarding three Jewish practices that Christians still follow: prayer, fasting, and almsgiving. These practices are centrally located in the sermon because they are central to living the life in Christ. Along with gathering for worship, prayer, fasting, and almsgiving are the basic, defining practices we undertake as disciples of Christ. This is because the Christian life is directed toward three focal points: God, our neighbor, and our soul. Like the needle of a compass, prayer orients our lives toward God; almsgiving turns our gaze to our neighbor. Fasting, on the other hand, directs our attention to ourselves.

Fasting is seldom mentioned in the New Testament—not because the practice was discouraged or ignored by the biblical writers, but because it was assumed. Fasting is most often encountered in the writings of St. Luke. Unlike the Gospels of Mark and Matthew, it seems Luke's Gospel was written during a relatively peaceful time in the life of the Church. His Gospel is concerned more with the everyday life of Christians, which includes fasting.

Luke notes that Anna remained in the temple in continual prayer and fasting (2:36–37). In Acts, he twice describes the Church as fasting (Acts 13:2–3; 14:23). In every instance when Luke mentions fasting, he links it with prayer. It is part of what the Old Testament calls the "fear of the Lord"—in other words, it is one way to express that we take God, and the things concerned with God, seriously.

FROM THE OUTSET, we should be clear what the Church means by fasting.

Most people understand a fast as an extended period of time when a person eats nothing. If, at the start of Lent, you announced to your friends you would be fasting for forty days, they would worry about you.

The fasting referred to in the New Testament and

by the earliest Church Fathers was this total fasting from food. This type of fasting stands behind Jesus' warning against showing off one's piety: "When you fast, do not be like the hypocrites, with a sad countenance. For they disfigure their faces that they may appear to men to be fasting. . . . When you fast, anoint your head and wash your face, so that you do not appear to men to be fasting" (Matt. 6:16–18).

Interestingly enough, fasting in this original sense is enjoying a comeback. People seeking to lose weight and otherwise improve their health, vitality, and cognitive abilities are turning to fasting. Numerous podcasts, blogs, and videos can easily be found promoting various schedules for IF (intermittent fasting) or touting the benefits of OMAD (one meal a day) for health and longevity. They have a point. When I first read the Sayings of the Desert Fathers, I thought the long lifespans attributed to some of these early monks was a pious exaggeration. Recent research suggests that their ages might have been reported accurately: caloric deprivation (i.e., fasting) seems to increase longevity.

When the Church's preparation for Pascha lengthened to forty days, a total fast became impossible. The Church's understanding of fasting came to include abstinence—restricting the kinds of food that were permitted. This is what, in *Great Lent*, Fr. Alexander Schmemann calls ascetical fasting: "a drastic reduction of food so that the permanent state of a certain hunger might live as a reminder of God and a constant effort to keep our mind on Him. Everyone who has practiced it knows that this ascetical fast rather than weakening us makes us light, concentrated, sober, joyful, pure."[1]

He continues, "Four times a year [the Church] invites us to purify and liberate ourselves from the dominion of the flesh by the holy therapy of fasting, and each time the success of the therapy depends precisely on the application of certain basic rules."[2]

What are the rules? Simply put, for the length of the fast Orthodox Christians become teetotaling vegans.

In actual practice, there are various (and welcome) modifications to the strict veganism of the longer fasts. For one, crustaceans are permitted. This may seem a puzzling exception until one recalls that things like shrimp, lobster, and crab were once considered insects. They were therefore blessed by the example of John the Forerunner, who ate only "locusts

---

1   Alexander Schmemann, *Great Lent* (Crestwood, NY: St. Vladimir's Seminary Press, 1969), 51.

2   Ibid, 98.

and wild honey."[3] Wine and fish are allowed on certain days, and exceptions or adjustments are always made for the sick and infirm, for pregnant or nursing women, and, of course, for children.

LIKE PRAYER AND ALMSGIVING, fasting is eminently practical—in the literal sense: it is something you put into practice, something you do. Putting this Christian discipline into practice in twenty-first–century North America presents its own set of difficulties. This book will attempt to face some of these difficulties while showing the continuing relevance and importance of practicing both fasting and other forms of Christian self-discipline.

---

3   Matthew 3:4. At least, that's my theory. It's an amusing historical footnote that Colonial-era prisoners in Connecticut's Newgate prison complained that being fed lobster every day was cruel and unusual punishment. Lobster did not become a luxury food until the twentieth century. It helps my case that in Maine, lobsters are referred to as "bugs."

PART I

Why We Fast

1

Because of Christ and the Church

First, we fast because Jesus clearly expected us to. As innumerable commentators over the centuries have pointed out, the text mentioned in the introduction (Matt. 6:16, which provides the title of this book), says *when,* not *if.* Our Lord clearly expected that His disciples would continue the Jewish practice of fasting.

The second reason is that the Church commands us to fast.

It's easy to miss how countercultural that statement is. It stands in complete opposition to contemporary American religiosity or spirituality. That someone might change his lifestyle or alter her eating habits if told to do so by their doctor is accepted. However, the idea that someone would do so simply because he or she had been told to do so by the Church would sound strange.

The garden-variety church-going American (an increasingly endangered species) treats church like a shopping mall. They are in the market for entertaining worship services, a nonjudgmental congregation, and sermons that are socially conscious and politically correct. Criteria such as sound doctrine, profoundly beautiful worship, and rigorous moral demands usually don't make the list.

When it comes to faith, most people pick and choose what they like from church and gospel and ignore the rest. There's even a name for such people: "cafeteria Christians." To be selected, a church must offer an "open and affirming," nonjudgmental attitude toward any "lifestyle choices" they've made. As far back as 1937, American theologian H. Reinhold Niebuhr summarized the American "gospel" thus: "A God without wrath [bringing] men without sin into a kingdom without judgment through the ministrations of a Christ without a cross."[4]

By contrast, the Orthodox Church offers a call to

---

4   H. Reinhold Niebuhr, *The Kingdom of God in America* (New York: Harper & Row, 1959 [1937]), 193.

repentance and conversion through self-denial and service. In a lecture, Fr. Thomas Hopko once summarized the gospel message this way: "If you want to be first, become the last; if you want to lead, become a servant; if you want to be rich, become poor; and if you want to live, die."

Twice a year—soon after the start of the liturgical new year and around six months later at the midpoint of Lent—Orthodox parishes enthrone a crucifix in the middle of their churches. The point is to remind us of Jesus' words, "If anyone desires to come after Me, let him deny himself, and take up his cross daily, and follow Me" (Luke 9:23).

Fasting, together with other forms of self-denial we will consider below, is a crucial component in the work of taking up our cross.

But the question remains, Why? There are (at least) three reasons:

✝ We fast to prepare.

✝ We fast to be free.

✝ We fast to be fruitful.

We Fast to Prepare

The Church calls us to fast before receiving Holy Communion as well as before Pascha and other important feasts. Father Alexander Schmemann notes that fasting "has been understood as a state of preparation and expectation—the state of spiritual concentration on that which is to come . . . the 'opening up' of the entire human being to the approaching joy."[5]

Fasting prepares us for more than sacraments and celebrations. Making small sacrifices for our faith is training for the day when we may have to suffer for our faith.

This is becoming more and more important. The days of comfortable discipleship in which our faith is appreciated and applauded, or in which it is even tolerated, are likely coming to an end. I don't mean to be alarmist or paranoid; I'm simply making an observation about the path our society has taken. In my lifetime I've seen popular opinion about the place and value of religion (particularly Christianity) and its portrayal in TV and film shift from respectful and supportive toward tolerant amusement, and then continue on to scorn, ridicule, and the increasing hostility evident now.

Active persecution, should it come, will likely first take the soft form of financial pressure applied not only on the institutional churches but on individuals.

---

5   *Great Lent*, 49.

Observers like Rod Dreher in *The Benedict Option* warn that financial consequences for faithfulness may be coming.

> The closure of certain professions to faithful orthodox Christians will be difficult to accept. . . . And many of us are not prepared to suffer deprivation for our faith. . . . Relearning asceticism—that is, how to suffer for the faith—is critical training for Christians living in the world today and the world of the near future.[6]

We Fast to Be Set Free

The second reason for embracing asceticism is to achieve freedom. Like truth, fasting will set us free.

That may sound strange. The Church's ascetic discipline, with the various sacrifices, obligations, and restrictions it imposes, does not look like freedom. Nonetheless, attaining freedom is the explicitly stated purpose for fasting.

In *The Lenten Triodion*—the book containing the liturgical texts for Lent and Holy Week—freedom is a recurring theme. The hymns of the *Triodion* portray human beings as people "who are enslaved by

---

6   Rod Dreher, *The Benedict Option* (New York: Penguin Publishing Group, 2017), 65.

the tyranny of the flesh."[7] These hymns poetically admonish us to take up asceticism as the key that will set us free: "Let us not be taken prisoner by our eyes; let not our tongue delight in costly food, for once they have been eaten they are worthless; let us shun all greed, then we shall not become slaves to the passions which follow an excess of food and drink."[8]

Father Alexander Schmemann puts it this way: "The purpose for fasting is to liberate man from the unlawful tyranny of the flesh, of that surrender of the spirit to the body and its appetite which is the tragical result of sin and the original fall of man."[9]

Spiritual liberation is central to the Church's experience of Lent because it is central to the historical experience of God's people. The foundational and defining historical event in both the Old and New Testaments is the Exodus, the act by which God freed His people from centuries of Egyptian bondage.

Because we Americans tend to confuse freedom with liberty, it's useful to note that there are actually three kinds of freedom: freedom *to*, freedom *from*, and freedom *for*. Each of these provides a theme for one of the three parts of Dante's epic poem, *The*

---

7   *The Lenten Triodion*, Vespers for the first Tuesday of Lent.
8   *Triodion*, 272.
9   *Great Lent*, 50.

Divine Comedy.[10] In the *Inferno* we see what results from the inordinate indulgence of our freedom *to.* The *Purgatorio* offers a literal as well as literary step-by-step guide to achieving freedom *from.* Finally, in the Paradiso we are given a glimpse of what human freedom is *for.*

Fasting and the other disciplines of abstinence are aimed at achieving freedom *from.* Dante's journey through Purgatory ends when, at last released from the prison of the seven deadly sins, he reenters Eden. Virgil, his teacher and guide, declares his independence: Whatever Dante wishes to do, he should do; his will and God's will are no longer in conflict. "Your judgment is now free and whole and true; to fail to follow its will would be to stray. Lord of yourself I crown and miter you."[11]

The freedom we can receive through asceticism is freedom from the passions. The vocabulary here is specific and technical: *passion* does not refer to intense, overwhelming emotion. Saint Ignatius Brianchaninov explains that "a sinful habit is called

---

10 This is an oversimplification, as Dante's epic explores multiple themes and incorporates just about everything medieval Europeans knew or thought, all in the midst of a riveting story.

11 Dante Alighieri, *Purgatory*, Canto Twenty-seven, Anthony Esolen, trans. (New York: The Modern Library, 2004), 297.

a passion (or vice); it deprives man of freedom and makes him a prisoner, a slave of sin and of the fallen angel."[12] The passions (the "toxic thoughts" identified by the earlier Fathers) make us helpless and passive in the struggle against sin. They multiply the suffering we endure and the pain we inflict on others. It is our tragedy that, having to live as fallen human beings, we abide in the condition of unfreedom.

Paradoxically, taking up the cross of asceticism is the way we can set down the heavy burden we all carry. It's as though you're lugging two heavy suitcases through the airport and suddenly spot your family running toward you. You drop your luggage and open your arms to receive the welcomed and welcoming embrace of those who love you.

We Fast to Be Fruitful

Fruitfulness is the Gospels' favorite metaphor for what our Lord expects to find in His Church and in the lives of His followers. Even before Jesus begins His ministry, we hear of it. On the banks of the Jordan, John the Forerunner challenges the Pharisees and Sadducees who have come to hear him to "bear

---

12   Bishop Ignatius Brianchaninov, *The Arena* (Jordanville, NY: Printshop of St. Job of Pochaev, 1997), 127.

fruits worthy of repentance" (Matt. 3:8). In Jesus' teaching, fruitfulness is a recurring metaphor. This takes a startling turn a few days before His death. Returning to Jerusalem hungry, Jesus looks for food on a fig tree. There is none. The evangelists point out that it is the wrong time of the year for figs; that doesn't matter. Jesus curses the fig tree, and it withers (Mark 11:19–24).

This scene, which on the surface portrays Jesus as petty and petulant, amounts to a performance parable. It echoes and expands the Forerunner's warning at the beginning of Luke's Gospel: "Even now the ax is laid to the root of the trees. Therefore, every tree which does not bear good fruit is cut down and thrown into the fire" (Luke 3:9). With this action, Jesus reveals that, with His coming, judgment has come to Jerusalem, and the criterion will be fruitfulness.

Metaphors are like jokes: explaining them doesn't help. They either work or they don't. You either get them or you don't. What may help in this case is contrasting fruits and products. Since the Industrial Revolution we've come to see the wares in our stores as products—even fruits and vegetables are called "produce." However, there is a difference. Manufacturing is a scientifically managed, mathematically measured process. The materials needed are listed and counted, the steps are sequenced and followed, and the end result is predictable and certain. Despite the best efforts of industrialized agriculture, however, differences still remain between the farm and the factory.

In the bearing of fruit, the result is neither swift, certain, nor guaranteed. A factory may be streamlined and made more efficient, but there are limits to how much this can be done with a field. Farm machinery shortens the time it takes to till the soil, plant the seed, and harvest the grain, but the growth from seed to grain cannot be rushed. Further, farmers can do all the right things assiduously, but bad weather, blight, or insects can still destroy the harvest. There remains an element of uncertainty and therefore of mystery. There is room for the workings of grace.

As Jesus observes, after a farmer scatters seed, though he does not know how, the seed sprouts and grows: "For the earth yields crops by itself: first the blade, then the head, after that the full grain in the head" (Mark 4:28).

Fruits of Repentance

What kind of fruit is Jesus looking for in His Church and in us?

The first answer is what John the Baptist called the "fruits worthy of repentance" (Luke 3:8). We have a tendency to imagine repentance and conversion as a quick and dramatic decision: The adulterous husband leaves his mistress, the alcoholic smashes his bottle on the sidewalk and finds an AA meeting. Scrooge wakes up on Christmas morning and, literally overnight, has been converted from miser to philanthropist.

The agricultural metaphor suggests otherwise. Conversion, Kathleen Norris reminds us, "is a process; it is not a goal, not a product we consume. And it's a bodily process, not only an emotional or intellectual one."[13] The process is slow and incremental. In Western monasticism, monks and nuns following the Rule of St. Benedict take a vow of *conversatio morum*—essentially a promise to pursue a lifelong conversion. A promise is demanded because the work is long, slow, and often discouraging. A lifetime is required for the same reason.

We have a clear idea of what we are to be converted from, but we also need to know what we are converting to. The key text for us is the Sermon on the Mount.

Numerous commentators have remarked that Matthew positions Jesus' Sermon on the Mount as

---

13 Kathleen Norris, *Amazing Grace: A Vocabulary of Faith* (New York: Riverhead Books, 1998), 41.

parallel to Moses giving the Torah to the Israelites at Mount Sinai. Both are set in a covenant context, and both provide an explicit statement of what that covenant requires. But Jesus raises the bar.

First of all, Jesus is putting His would-be followers on display in front of everyone. Picture the scene as set by Matthew (5:1): Jesus is teaching; His disciples are listening; and behind them the crowd is also listening. With each word, Jesus is telling His disciples what He expects from them and telling the crowd what they should expect from His disciples. He tells His followers they are to be like a hilltop city visible for miles, like lamps pushing back the darkness with good works that will lead others to glorify God.

Second, Jesus sets a higher moral standard than Moses did: "Unless your righteousness exceeds *the righteousness* of the scribes and Pharisees, you will by no means enter the kingdom of heaven" (5:20). Jesus targets earlier moral standards one after another, introducing each with the phrase, "You have heard that it was said to those of old . . . ," then lifting it to new heights with each "But I say to you . . ."

The line once drawn at murder is now drawn at anger. The banning of adulterous acts is strengthened by the forbidding of adulterous intentions. Divorce, oath-taking, and retaliation are out. Jesus sums it up by saying "You shall be perfect, just as your Father in heaven is perfect" (5:48). With these words, He makes it clear that His aim is nothing less than restoring to humanity the image and likeness of God that were lost.

So what should the world expect to find in the Church? What does Christ want to find in us? It's all there in Jesus' words: the thirst for justice combined with the work of peacemaking; enduring persecution with forgiving our persecutors; the life freed from worldly worries because greater store is set in heaven; prayer, fasting, and almsgiving quietly continuing; going the extra mile and turning the other cheek. All performed with a conspicuous absence of Jonah-like passive-aggression or pharisaical self-aggrandizement.

So where does fasting fit in? The answer can be found in the best-known "agricultural" parable, variously called "The Sower and the Seed" or "The Four Soils."

There is bad news here. Fruitfulness can be stifled by the world, the flesh, or the devil—as shown in the first three soils. There is also good news: soil can be improved. When a landowner, frustrated that a fig tree has not produced any fruit in years, orders it cut down, his keeper suggests, "Sir, let it alone this year also, until I dig around it and fertilize *it*. And if it bears fruit, *well*. But if not, after that you can cut it down" (Luke 13:8–9).

In one chapter of *The Arena*, St. Ignatius Brianchaninov takes the tilling of the soil as a metaphor for asceticism. He writes that "to till the earth, various iron tools and implements are needed. . . . So too our heart . . . needs cultivation by fasting, watching, vigils, prostrations and other oppressions of the body."[14] He continues:

> The man who would take it into his head to cultivate his land without using farm implements would . . . labor in vain. Just so, he who wants to acquire virtues without bodily discipline will labor in vain. . . . Likewise, a man who is always ploughing his land without ever seeding it will reap nothing. Just so, he who is incessantly occupied merely with bodily discipline will be unable to practice spiritual exercises, such as planting in his heart the commandments of the Gospel, which in due time would bear spiritual fruits.[15]

Much is at stake here.

---

14   *Arena*, 137.
15   *Arena*, 138.

Although, as noted above, we are contending with a determinedly secularized education system, hostile news media, and a scornful entertainment industry, it is ultimately believers' lack of spiritual fruit that is undermining the Church's witness to the world. The fruits of the Holy Spirit as listed by St. Paul—love, joy, peace, longsuffering, kindness, goodness, faithfulness, gentleness, and self-control—must be noticeably present in our lives (see Gal. 5:22–23). Otherwise, people seeking an alternative to what our culture is offering will not consider the Church as an option.

To fail to bring forth the fruits of repentance is to fail Christ and to fail the world.

FINALLY, the foregoing should make it clear that fasting has a missionary aspect. God's response to the evil and suffering around us is *us*. We are the forces our Lord has deployed to help and heal. Saint Paul repeatedly refers to the Church as the Body of Christ. The Church is the sacrament of Christ's continuing, active presence in the world. The Holy Spirit's work of grafting diverse people into one Body amounts to an extension and expansion in time and space of our Lord's Incarnation. This places a cross on our shoulders, a burden of responsibility for each other and for the world.

Through asceticism and self-discipline, we voluntarily submit ourselves to something, to someone, greater than ourselves. By transcending our desires or preferences, we achieve escape velocity and break free from the constricting orbit of our ego. Doing this is crucial if we are going to live holy and fruitful lives as disciples of Christ. It is the way we shoulder the cross each of us has been given.

PART II

How We Fast

2

Fast with the Church

First of all, we fast with the Church. In practice, this means we fast when the Church fasts. Fasting is not something we do by ourselves or for ourselves—we fast as part of a community on appointed days (often marked on our parish calendars) and during specified seasons.

Experts in time management and productivity recommend that we take the items on our to-do list and move them into our calendars. They advise us to make appointments with ourselves to tackle these tasks; otherwise our lists are simply a collection of good intentions and our goals only idle dreams. Because fasting is important, the Church does the same thing: fasting (like prayer) is a regularly scheduled activity.

In its first decades, the Church adopted and modified the Jewish practice of fasting twice a week. The earliest document we have outside the New Testament, the *Didache*, records that Christians fasted on Wednesdays and Fridays.[16] This was a rescheduling of what had become a widespread Jewish practice by Jesus' day. Pious Jews fasted on Monday and Thursday—two days after and two days before the Sabbath.

The first Christians shifted the days in order to distinguish themselves from the Pharisees. They chose Wednesday because it was the day when Judas offered to betray Jesus, and Friday because it was the day of Jesus' Crucifixion. They were taking literally Jesus' saying that "the days will come when the bridegroom will be taken away from them; then they will fast in those days" (Luke 5:35).

The *Didache* also commands that "before the baptism let the baptiser and him who is to be baptized fast, and any others who are able. And thou shalt bid him who is to be baptized to fast one or two days before."[17] Since baptisms were typically done just before Pascha, this is the origin of Lenten fasting. At

---

16   Also known as "The Teaching of the Holy Apostles," the *Didache* is partly contemporary with the Gospels of Matthew and Luke. Fasting is discussed in section VIII.

17   Ibid.

its core, Lent was about preparing the catechumens for baptism and the community to receive its new members.

Today, and for well over a thousand years, the Orthodox Church's schedule for fasting has been:

✠ Wednesdays and Fridays

✠ Lent and Holy Week

✠ The forty days before Christmas (often called "Advent")

✠ The two weeks before the feast of the Dormition of the Theotokos (August 1–14 NC, August 14–27 OC)

✠ The Apostles' Fast, which starts eight days after Pentecost and continues until the feast of Saints Peter and Paul on June 29/July 12

✠ Isolated fast days such as the Exaltation of the Cross and the memorial of the Beheading of St. John the Forerunner.

In a typical year, an Orthodox Christian is expected to fast for roughly half the days of the year.

Fasting days and seasons, and the changes they bring to our routines, play a crucial role in discipleship. However, they make up only half the picture. Feasting is as much a part of the rhythm of the Church's liturgical life as fasting. As much as food is used as a means of remembrance and repentance, it is also one of the means chosen for rejoicing and celebration.

In the Old Testament, the week ended with a Sabbath, a day for rest, and the year was punctuated with feasts where the people were told to "do no customary work" (Num. 28 & 29). The commandments scheduling days for communal celebration and feasting were as serious as the commandment to keep the Sabbath or to fast on the Day of Atonement. They were to be strictly obeyed without exception and without excuse.

There is a rhythm to our life in the Church. In the life we lead from week to week we maintain a steady, moderate level of work, reading, exercise, prayer, etc. But from time to time we intensify our efforts. One thing becomes the main thing. Other tasks or projects are postponed or ignored so that as much energy and attention as possible may be given to one goal or one project. Then we relax and rejoice, and finally return to our routine. The Church's calendar functions the same way. Our baseline is the weekly fasts on Wednesday and Friday, along with eucharistic celebration on Sunday. Then, at set times of the year for a predetermined length of time, the Church bids us to increase and intensify our effort and focus drastically on both fasting and feasting.

One result of this is that we become more firmly

welded together into a community. In the language of St. Paul, we are "edified," both personally and as a Church: "As you therefore have received Christ Jesus the Lord, so walk in Him, rooted and built up [edified] in Him and established in the faith, as you have been taught, abounding in it with thanksgiving" (Col. 2:6–7).

Times of fasting are training sessions for the Body of Christ. Men and women in the military endure intense hardship while training and much worse in combat. Besides preparing them for the hazards they may face, training forges a haphazard collection of individuals into a cohesive unit. In a similar way, Peter urges the Christians to whom he is writing to stand firm in the face of suffering for their faith, "knowing that the same sufferings are experienced by your brotherhood in the world" (1 Peter 5:9). While fasting hardly measures up to the ordeals of suffering persecution, military training, or combat, it works the same way: it deepens our union with each other and our communion with Christ.

3

Choose Your Weapons

There's more to fasting than fasting.

The word "fasting" is shorthand for the entire range of disciplines Christians have undertaken for centuries. For the Church, these are the tools, or more accurately, the weapons we use in our largely unseen warfare against the kingdom of Satan, the kingdoms of this world, and the kingdom of self.

Unseen Warfare was the title chosen in the nineteenth century by St. Theophan the Recluse for his translation into Russian of Lorenzo Scupoli's book *Spiritual Combat.* In his foreword, St. Theophan writes of "the unseen and inner struggle, which every Christian undertakes from the moment of his baptism, when he makes a vow to God to fight for him, to the glory of His Name, even unto death."[18] He goes on to cite St. Paul: "We do not wrestle against flesh and blood, but against principalities, against powers, against the rulers of the darkness of this age, against spiritual *hosts* of wickedness in the heavenly *places*" (Eph. 6:12).

After prayer, fighting this fight is the most valuable service the Church offers the world, and it is the mission of everyone who follows Christ. This point is dramatically illustrated by Terrence Malick's visually stunning 2019 movie, *A Hidden Life*. The film tells the true story of Franz Jägerstätter, a devout Austrian Catholic who was martyred during World War II for refusing to take a loyalty oath to Hitler. Malick ends his film with the closing line of George Eliot's masterpiece, *Middlemarch*: "The growing good of the world is partly dependent on unhistoric acts; and that things are not so ill with you and me as they might have been is half owing to the number who lived faithfully a hidden life, and rest in unvisited tombs."[19]

Fasting, in the wider sense, cannot be optional for us. In *The Lenten Spring*, Fr. Thomas Hopko insists,

---

18 Theophan the Recluse, *Unseen Warfare* (Crestwood, NY: St. Vladimir's Seminary Press, 1978), 71.

19 George Eliot, *Middlemarch* (1871). George Eliot was the pen name of Mary Ann Evans.

"A human being must fast. The effort enlightens the mind, strengthens the spirit, controls the emotions and tames the passions."[20] Philosopher Joseph Pieper reminds his readers that fasting is a "natural, fundamental moral obligation," one that enables us to "become what we are by essence: the free moral person in full possession of himself."[21]

Dallas Willard, a Protestant philosophy professor, has presented a list of fifteen classical Christian disciplines which, he insists, all Christians need to practice.[22] He sorts them into two categories, which he calls the "Disciplines of Abstinence" and the "Disciplines of Engagement." Christian engagement includes such practices as worship and prayer, study, and service. Along with fasting, the disciplines of abstinence include solitude and silence, self-restraint through frugality and chastity, and sacrifice—all performed in secrecy.

These disciplines are the equipment we have been issued by the Church for our spiritual struggle. They are provided to help us build a life that is of service to

---

20 Thomas Hopko, *The Lenten Spring* (Crestwood, NY: St. Vladimir's Seminary Press, 1983), 109.

21 Josef Pieper, *The Four Cardinal Virtues* (Notre Dame, IN: University of Notre Dame Press, Kindle Edition), 178.

22 Dallas Willard, *The Spirit of the Disciplines: Understanding How God Changes Lives* (New York: Harper One, 1988).

our neighbors and pleasing to God. These disciplines are our weapons in our resistance campaign against the three enemies of grace—the age in which we live (the world), our own fallen human nature (the flesh), and the one who wields these against us (the devil). The Church calls the proper and effective use of these weapons *asceticism*.

This word has become problematic. Today, the word "ascetic" brings to the minds of many the picture of an emaciated hermit with a fondness for self-flagellation. In our self-indulgent times, Christian asceticism makes an easy target for derision. For instance, it has been mocked, scorned, and misrepresented in popular culture by such books and films as *Monty Python and the Holy Grail*, *The Name of the Rose*, and *The Da Vinci Code*.

The picture is false. Jesus admonishes us, in effect, to wash our faces and comport ourselves with a cheerful demeanor when fasting. Some mistakenly see fasting as something remarkable and heroic—and reserved for saints. On the contrary, Jesus' words imply that fasting (and the other forms of ascesis) are a normal, even mundane, part of the life of the typical Christian.

The word "asceticism" is rooted in the Greek word *ascesis*, which means "exercise, training." It should bring to mind the image of a determined athlete rigorously preparing to compete. This is what St. Paul has in mind when he writes in his first letter to Corinth:

> Do you not know that those who run in a race all run, but one receives the prize? Run in such a way that you may obtain *it*. And everyone who competes *for the prize* is temperate in all things. Now they *do it* to obtain a perishable crown, but we *for* an imperishable *crown*. Therefore I run thus: not with uncertainty. Thus I fight: not as *one who* beats the air. But I discipline my body and bring *it* into subjection, lest, when I have preached to others, I myself should become disqualified. (1 Cor. 9:24–27)

Since a short book must necessarily limit its focus, silence will take center stage next to fasting in the pages that follow. Not because the other ascetic practices Willard lists are less important, but rather because they are not as universally applicable. When St. John the Baptist was preaching, people from various walks of life came to him, asking, "What should we do?" St. John tailored his responses to each person (Luke 3:10–14). Each one of us is called to a unique life, and what will provide the most help for our struggle will be different for each person and will change at various points in our life.

How do we know which to choose?

✜ First, since fasting and silence (discussed below) are the foundational practices, these should be our starting point. We undertake these before any of the others.

✜ Second, we use the Church's calendar of fast days as a schedule of our efforts.

✜ Third, we seek guidance from others: our priest, or perhaps some other, more experienced Christian who knows us.

✜ Finally, we learn from our own experience. As St. Seraphim advised someone seeking his guidance, we must be like wise merchants, choosing what brings us the most profit.

4

Avoid Extremes

Serge Verhovskoy, former professor of dogmatic theology at St. Vladimir's Seminary, defined orthodoxy as "the absence of one-sidedness." His context was Christological. To overemphasize either the humanity or the divinity of Jesus was to become mired in heresy. I've since learned that avoiding one-sidedness is a principle with broader applications. There is wisdom here that provides guidance for following Jesus and for living a well-lived life.

Avoiding one-sidedness is difficult. Its opposite, extremism, is much easier. Once we've settled into an extreme position, we can relax. On the other hand, avoiding extremes is the mental equivalent of driving a car or riding a bike. Staying on course or keeping our balance requires constantly making micro-adjustments. Life, including an ascetic life (to the degree we are called to live it), demands the same diligence. Jesus describes the path to life as a narrow one (Matt. 7:13–14). Narrow paths are precarious; one misstep and we can lose our balance and fall to one side or the other.

One-sidedness is as much a danger in orthopraxis (right practice) as in orthodoxy (right doctrine). Orthodox teachers identify the two extremes to be avoided as excess and neglect,[23] or, in other words, nominalism and pharisaism. We must avoid both.

Nominalism

Nominalism is the desire to get through a fast with the minimum possible effort. We don't want the fasting lifestyle to disrupt our regular lifestyle too much. This happens especially when we start thinking of the Church as a social club with strict membership requirements. Lent, fasting, and the other ascetic disciplines are the unavoidable price of membership. We're willing to pay our dues, but we don't want them to be too expensive or inconvenient.

One recalls the Old Testament's master of

---

23   *Arena*, 138.

passive-aggressive compliance, the prophet Jonah. His assignment, the city of Nineveh, is described as being "an exceedingly great city"—so large that it would take three days to walk across it (Jonah 3:3). Jonah very deliberately walks for one day: one-third of the way into the city. Not one-fourth: that might not be enough for God to stop bothering him. Nor does he walk to the center of the city. He goes just far enough (he hopes) to say he obeyed.

In the section of *Great Lent* entitled "Taking It Seriously," Fr. Schmemann laments that "Although Lent is still 'observed' it has lost much of its impact on our lives. . . . The real root of [this] . . . is our conscious or unconscious reduction of religion to a superficial nominalism and symbolism . . . to explain away the 'seriousness' of religion's demands on our lives, religion's demands for commitment and effort."[24]

To borrow St. Paul's words, with nominalism we have a form of godliness but a denial of its real power (2 Tim. 3:5).

Pharisaism

The other extreme is to take our fasting too seriously, to become too focused on the minutiae of the rules or

---

the ingredients label on the box. Saint Ignatius Brianchaninov calls this "excess." The risk here is that we will use fasting to establish our own righteousness (i.e., self-righteousness) rather than seeking "the righteousness which is from God" (Phil. 3:9). This attitude gets the name "pharisaism" from the overly meticulous Pharisees, whom Jesus chided for tithing even mint, dill, and cumin while neglecting the weightier matters of the law (Matt. 23:23).

Saint Ignatius warns that "excess . . . is just as harmful, or even more so, then neglect."[25] He famously describes monks who

> attribute special significance to dry bread, mushrooms, cabbages, peas or beans, [thus] easy, sensible, and holy spiritual exercises [are] turned into senseless, carnal and sinful farces, the ascetic [is] corrupted and reduced to . . . conceit and contempt for his neighbors which snuffs out the very conditions for progress in holiness.[26]

Because this snare has been set, even before the start of Lent, we are reminded in the *Lenten Triodion,*

---

25   *Arena,* 138.
26   *Arena,* 195.

"In vain do you rejoice in not eating . . . the demons never eat."[27]

How can we avoid extremity? By keeping the goal of fasting in mind.

Asceticism is goal-oriented. Fasting, and all the other Christian disciplines, are tools invented for specific purposes. Just as hammers drive nails and pulleys hoist weights, asceticism is intended to increase our willingness and capacity to love God and our neighbor. If our efforts do not move us closer to this goal, they are wasted and we "perform a useless fast."

As Fr. Schmemann reminds us, "we need first of all a spiritual preparation for the effort of fasting. It consists in making our fasting God-centered. We should fast for God's sake."[28]

---

27   Matins of Cheesefare Wednesday.
28   *Great Lent*, 97.

5

Start with Food

As we remarked above, the Gospel of Luke seems more focused on the day-to-day living of the Christian life than the other three Gospels were able to be. In its pages, we are more likely to find Jesus at prayer or at a meal. The frequent appearance of women in the narrative establishes a domestic tone. Care for the poor, the sick, and the helpless is a recurring theme. It is not surprising, then, that when Luke records Jesus' words about bearing one's cross, he includes the word "daily" (Luke 9:23).

Bearing our cross and denying ourselves are necessary for following Christ. They are instrumental for the lifelong process one contemporary monastic writer calls "submitting the totality of our lives to progressive evangelization."[29]

We can see how this works in *The Screwtape Letters*, when C. S. Lewis's titular demon warns his protégé that God is working to bring about the "patient's" ever-expanding conversion: "The Enemy [God] will be working from the centre outward, gradually bringing more and more of the patient's conduct under the new standard, and may reach his behavior to [his mother] at any moment."[30]

What is our part in this process? How do we cooperate with God's grace? Where do we start?

We start with food.

Change your eating and you change your life. Your life will be different in very real and practical ways. This is not a particularly spiritual or specifically Christian insight; it is a universal human experience. What we eat, how much we eat, and when we eat affects how we feel and how we think, how we act and how we interact. When we change what we eat for the sake of following Christ, our life in Christ changes.

---

29 Michael Casey, *Sacred Reading* (Liguori, MI: Liguori Press, 1995), 74.

30 C. S. Lewis, *The Screwtape Letters* (New York: Harper Collins, 2000), 11.

It's easy to think that changing what and how we eat occupies such a low position on the scale of importance that making even a temporary change is scarcely worth the inconvenience. Menu planning, shopping, and cooking, like our other menial chores, are tedious and boring. We file conversations about them under "small talk." The day-to-day chores of life are barely noticed and rarely remembered. No one posts pictures of themselves doing the dishes or taking out the trash on social media.

Nonetheless, we greatly underestimate the impact of everyday routines. Consider that Jesus taught us to pray for our daily bread, and then shortly afterward admonished us not to pile tomorrow's anxieties onto today's plate of worry: "Sufficient for the day *is* its own trouble" (Matt. 6:34). We are to focus on the now because, as C. S. Lewis notes, "the Present is the point at which time touches eternity."[31] However humdrum and unexciting they may seem, we must take everyday things with the utmost seriousness. They are important precisely because we do them every day.

One thing we do every day is eat. It keeps us alive; it makes us feel better. Food's reach extends beyond

---

31   *Screwtape*, 75.

the physiological and psychological. On a purely material level, the bare fact that we must eat connects us to a complex political, social, economic, and ecological network that stretches across centuries, continents, and species. While these connections are not the focus of this book, they are implicit in all that will be said here. Food connects us to the web of life, which in turn is the locus of Christ's redeeming work. The Church reveals her overarching purpose for fasting in the psalm verse chosen to mark the liturgical inauguration of Lent: "Seek God, and your soul shall live" (Psalm 68:33).

Building a Bridge

Because food is so essential for life, the Church uses fasting to construct a bridge between our faith and our life. Just as the divine Word became flesh in the body of Jesus (John 1:14), so must God's revealed word become flesh—become real, present, and active through our bodies.

This has become crucial. We live in what has been called "the Age of Feelings."[32] The world around us

---

32   An important term coined by Princeton Law Professor Robert P. George to distinguish our times from what Will and Ariel Durant called "the Age of Faith" (the Middle Ages) and "the Age of Reason" (the Enlightenment).

believes that we are what we feel, and if we speak and act accordingly we are "being authentic." Possessing or professing the right sentiments spares us the trouble of taking action. This is nothing new. In the first century, St. James had to warn his readers, "If a brother or sister is naked and destitute of daily food, and one of you says to them, 'Depart in peace, be warmed and filled,' but you do not give them the things which are needed for the body, what *does it* profit? Thus also faith by itself, if it does not have works, is dead" (James 2:15–17).

Generous feelings, caring thoughts, and kind words are not enough. Our will and our actions matter more. This is why Jesus' Sermon on the Mount ends with words of warning: "Not everyone who says to Me, 'Lord, Lord,' shall enter the kingdom of heaven, but he who does the will of My Father in heaven" (Matt. 7:21).

One of the things we do to move our discipleship from mere church attendance or lip service into the reality of action is fasting.

Taking Action

Fasting should simplify our shopping, meal planning, and cooking, not complicate it. When we fast, we are supposed to be moving the needle closer to the example of Mary of Bethany, but if we are not vigilant, we end up wrenching it over to Martha mode. Jesus told Martha, "But one thing is needed" (Luke 10:42). We should apply this to fasting. These are the days to simplify the food we serve, wash fewer dishes, and save our time and money for other things.

As much as possible, follow the Church's fasting discipline noted above. But anticipate and accept that health, work, family, and personal life may require you to lower the bar. It's nothing to agonize about, but it's also nothing to be done lightly or on a whim. First check with your parish priest, whose job it is to hold you accountable.

And in general:

☩ Eat less.

☩ Eat less often.

☩ Eat simply.

☩ Don't eat out if you can avoid it.

☩ Be bored by your menu from time to time.

☩ Think about food less often.

☩ Feel, and endure feeling, hunger at some point in your day.

☩ Spend less on groceries and give what you save to the poor.

✠ Remember, if it's not an effort, it's not a fast.

Remember, too, what St. Ignatius Brianchaninov reminds us of in *The Arena*: "Fasting is a primary instrument of all the virtues."[33]

---

33   *Arena*, 135.

6

Deny Yourself

All the disciplines of abstinence listed above involve some form of self-denial. To practice self-denial is to choose voluntarily not to do things we want to do. It is saying no to our whims, impulses, and preferences. It means refusing to surrender to our craving for instant self-gratification. It is to set out on the path philosophers have called the *via negativa*.

Via Negativa

An often-repeated story says that, when Michelangelo was asked how he had carved his statue of David, he answered, "I removed everything that was not David." While the truth of the story is dubious, it nonetheless illustrates what is meant by via negativa.

Like sculpting, the disciplines of abstinence work by a slow and sometimes painstaking process of subtraction. The outcome will be the removal of all that distorts or obscures God's likeness in us.

Via negativa translates as "negative path" or the "way of negation." In Orthodoxy it is often referred to as "apophaticism." In Orthodox theology it first refers to the church councils' struggle to find language to express, without misleadings or misgivings, what it meant by the doctrine of the Holy Trinity. The work began by clarifying what was not meant: not three gods, not three parts of God, not three roles played by God, but three Persons. We meet apophatic expression again in the eucharistic prayer of St. John Chrysostom. God is glorified as "ineffable, inconceivable, incomprehensible"—beyond words, beyond thought, beyond understanding.

In the pagan world, the via negativa provided ethical guidelines for virtuous living. Its most famous expression is found in the Hippocratic oath: First, do no harm. It finds expression also in what has been called the "Silver Rule." This flip side to the Golden Rule directs us not to do to others what we would not want them to do to us. Sometimes it's the only path open to us. Even if we find ourselves in a situation where nothing we can do or say will make things better, it is still within our power at least not to make things worse.

The great example of via negativa is God's Covenant with His people. Most of the Ten Commandments are expressed in negative terms—the "thou shalt nots"—the things we are not to do. Later, in Leviticus, the list expands to include the holiness code—injunctions that clarify the ways God's people will stand apart from their neighbors. The list ranges from the profound to the puzzling: no idols, no human sacrifices—and no boiling a goat in its mother's milk. In Leviticus, to be holy meant to be different, and being different meant not doing what the Gentiles did. It meant via negativa.

The Battle of Wills

The point of human life—and therefore the aim of all our striving—is the love of God. When Jesus was asked what the greatest commandment was, He gave the same answer any Jew would: "Hear, O Israel, the Lord our God, the Lord is one. And you shall love the Lord your God with all your heart, with all your soul, with all your mind, and with all your strength" (Mark 12:29–30). The truth of our love for God is shown in our fulfillment of the commandments of Christ: "If you love Me, keep My commandments" (John 14:15). Luke would probably have added the word "daily" to the end of that sentence, too. The whole point, therefore, of Christian asceticism is to increase our capacity to obey Christ.

We can trace a direct line across the pages of the Gospels from Mary's "Behold the maidservant of the Lord! Let it be to me according to your word" (Luke 1:38) to Jesus in the Garden of Gethsemane ending His prayer for deliverance with "Not My will, but Yours, be done" (Luke 22:42). The line extends to us when we pray "Thy will be done."

Here we run into a problem—or rather, *the* problem. It is what Tito Colliander in *The Way of the Ascetics* calls our "unchecked habit of satisfying only our own will."[34] Because we are fallen human beings living in a fallen world, the tragic reality is that our will and God's will are frequently in conflict.

Saint Paul summed up the human condition when he wrote, "what I will to do, that I do not practice; but what I hate, that I do. . . . I know that in me (that is, in my flesh) nothing good dwells. . . . [The way] to perform what is good I do not find. For the good that I will *to do*, I do not do; but the evil I will not *to do*, that I practice" (Rom. 7:15, 18–19).

---

34   Tito Colliander, *The Way of the Ascetics* (New York: St. Vladimir's Seminary Press, 1985), 13.

Too often, we find ourselves on a seesaw where to do God's will we must stop doing our own. To raise God's will above our own, we must push our will down to the level of the earth; to serve our neighbor, we must be less self-serving. An ancient play on words is at work here. The word "humility" comes from the word *humus*—fertile soil. Practicing humility means exalting our God and elevating our neighbor above ourselves by lowering ourselves. Therefore, we are called to self-denial; therefore, we practice the disciplines of abstinence.

Denying Ourselves Daily

The opportunities for self-denial God sends us each day are actionable, specific, and within our capacities (see 1 Cor. 10:13). Like any form of training, they move us incrementally closer to our goal. We may not be able to give thanks at all times for all things, but we can stop complaining. We may lack the courage to speak the truth when it is risky, but we can refuse to say anything we know is untrue.

In *The Way of the Ascetics*, Tito Colliander suggests we should occasionally exercise self-denial in small things just for practice: "If you have the urge to ask for something, don't ask! If you have the urge to drink two cups of coffee, drink only one! If you wish to smoke a cigarette, refrain! If you want to go visiting, stay at home!"[35]

We cannot say "yes" without first saying "no." Self-denial is the cost of following Christ. It is the "no" that makes every other "yes" possible.

35   *Way of the Ascetics*, 14.

7

Talk Less

Examining all the disciplines of abstinence is beyond the scope of a short book like this one. There is, however, one ascetic practice that provides greater leverage than all the others.

If a survey were taken of biblical and patristic authors asking them to choose one other discipline to be universally recommended, the answer would be unanimous. It would be "silence." Restricting what we let come out of our mouth, they would agree, is even more important than controlling what we put into it.

Listing all the verses in the Bible that urge us to watch what we say, or to stay silent altogether, would be a lengthy exercise. This call for silence has been repeated by spiritual writers in every century. One recent example is Fr. Thomas Hopko's "Fifty-five Maxims for the Christian Life." Thirteen of the fifty-five deal directly or indirectly with practicing silence or restraining our speech.

If anything, in our day the value of silence has increased a thousandfold. Few things are so notably absent today as the absence of words.

There are three kinds of silence: interior, exterior, and environmental (discussed in the next chapter).

Interior silence refers to the quieting of our inner thoughts. Orthodox ascetic writers call it *hesychia*—stillness, silence. *Hesychasm*, what we call the practice of the prayer of the heart that centers on the Jesus Prayer, comes from this word.

The second category, exterior silence, refers to speech. It is the silence most frequently urged by biblical writers, particularly in the wisdom literature of the Old Testament and in the Epistle of St. James. What these writers advise is easy to summarize: Say as little as possible, and watch what you say.

Not surprisingly, the importance of exterior silence is also stressed in Christian monasticism. When St. Anthony of Egypt, the founder of this way of life, was asked by another monk, "What ought I to do?" he replied, "Do not trust in your own righteousness, do not worry about the past, but control your tongue and your stomach."[36]

The grace of saying less is frequently sought in prayer. Every evening for nearly three thousand years, God's people have prayed, "Set a watch, O Lord, before my mouth, / A door of enclosure about my lips" (Psalm 140/141:3). During Lent the frequently recited Prayer of St. Ephraim includes a petition to escape the spirit of "idle talk." Saint Ephraim uses the Greek word *aglaria* here. Some translators also suggest "useless talk" or "vain babbling" as the English equivalent. It is what the late Dartmouth professor Donald Sheehan, in his reflection on this prayer, called "speech that has no capacity to achieve work . . . speech that achieves nothing."[37] Victory over our own uncontrolled indulgence in this kind of speech is one of the things we should be praying for.

The Church stands in agreement with the wisdom taught for thousands of years around the world: Silence is a virtue, and it should be practiced by all who wish to become wise and good and virtuous.

The first reason for this is that silence helps us

36   Benedicta Ward, *The Sayings of the Desert Fathers* (Kalamazoo, MI: Cistercian Publications, 1975), 2.

37   Donald Sheehan, *The Grace of Incorruption* (Brewster, MA: Paraclete Press, 2015), 15.

avoid sin. One of the desert fathers, St. Arsenius, recalled that he had "often repented for having spoken, but never for having kept silent."[38] So many of the words we speak on any given day are mostly used to impress or to dominate others, to prove we are right, or to get our own way. The Book of Proverbs warns us that "you will not escape sin by a multitude of words" (10:19).

Silence is the necessary prerequisite for listening to our God and our neighbor. The God of the Bible is the God who speaks. Eight times in Deuteronomy, the people are commanded to "Hear, O Israel." The Israelites stand amazed and terrified that God speaks to them: "Surely the Lord our God has shown us His glory and His greatness, and we heard His voice from the midst of the fire. We saw this day that God speaks with man; yet [the man] still lives" (5:24).

Listening is basic to discipleship. A disciple is not just a follower; a disciple is a student. For this reason, when we gather with our fellow disciples for Liturgy, one of the first acts of worship is listening to the reading of Scripture. In the West, St. Benedict's monastic rule famously begins with the invitation to

---

38 Found in many places, notably in Benedicta Ward's *The Desert Fathers: Sayings of the Early Christian Monks* (New York: Penguin Classics, 2003).

"Listen carefully, my son, to the master's instructions, and attend to them with the ear of your heart."[39] If we listen, we learn. If we practice silence, we grow in wisdom and knowledge. And, when we do speak, our words will exalt rather than humble, heal rather than hurt, guide rather than deceive, and encourage rather than afflict.

How Is It done?

We start by admitting that for some of us (certainly for me) exterior silence is hard to practice and rarely achieved. Nonetheless, it is something we work toward.

This undertaking, like all our other work, relies on prayer. To Psalm 140/141:3 (quoted above) and the Prayer of St. Ephraim, we can add the petition from the Prayer at Daybreak by Elder (now Saint) Sophrony of Essex:

> By the power of your blessing enable me
> at all times to speak and to act with a pure
> spirit to your glory. . . . Preserve me from
> every word and act which corrupts the soul,

---

39 Timothy Fry, *The Rule of St. Benedict in English* (Collegeville, MN: Liturgical Press, 1981), 15. It should be noted that, after the Bible, St. Benedict's Rule became the fundamental and foundational text of Western Civilization.

and from every impulse that is unpleasing in your sight and harmful to the people around me. Teach me what I should say and how I should speak. If it be your holy will that I be quiet and make no answer, inspire me to be silent in a peaceful spirit that causes neither harm nor hurt to my fellow human beings.[40]

Next, on Wednesdays and Fridays at least, we should make an effort to control both the quantity and quality of our speech. This means that, as much as we can and as often as we remember, we say as few words as we can without attracting attention. It also means that when conversation is unavoidable (as it often will be) we endeavor to say less about ourselves, to ask more questions, and to really listen to the answers.

Sometimes we find good advice in unlikely places. A meme on the internet urges people to "THINK before you speak." THINK is an acronym. Before we say anything, it recommends we first ask ourselves if what we are about to say is True, Helpful, Inspiring, Necessary, or Kind. If our words do not meet at least one, and preferably more than one, of these criteria, they should not pass our lips.

---

40 Originally published in Sophrony Sakharov, *His Life Is Mine* (Crestwood, NY: St. Vladimir's Seminary Press, 1977).

8

Cultivate Silence

To practice asceticism is to engage in subversion. Ascetic disciplines quietly call into question much of what our culture considers important. Practicing ascesis runs counter to accepted and expected behavior in our society (or any society, for that matter). This is especially true of the ascetic effort to establish a degree of environmental silence in our life.

Designating certain hours (or, more likely, moments) in our schedule to spend quiet times in silent spaces has never been more difficult—or more important. Indeed, to do this is nothing less than taking defensive action against the demonic. In one letter, C. S. Lewis's epistolary demon Screwtape gleefully gloats:

Music and silence—how I detest them both!
How thankful we should be that ever since
our Father entered Hell—though longer ago
than humans, reckoning in light years, could
express—no square inch of infernal space
and no moment of infernal time has been
surrendered to either of those abominable
forces, but all has been occupied by Noise—
Noise, the grand dynamism, the audible
expression of all that is exultant, ruthless,
and virile—Noise which alone defends us
from silly qualms, despairing scruples, and
impossible desires. We will make the whole
universe a noise in the end. We have already
made great strides in this direction as regards
the Earth. The melodies and silences of
Heaven will be shouted down in the end.[41]

Half a century ago, Fr. Schmemann wrote that
although "the Christian of the past lived in a great
measure in a silent world, giving him ample opportunity for concentration and inner life, today's Christian has to make a special effort to recover that essential dimension of silence which alone can put us in

---

41 *Screwtape,* 92–93.

contact with higher realities."[42] What would he have made of our current hyperconnected condition? We are constantly besieged by the culture of distraction that assaults our senses with content deliberately engineered to addict us.

Calls for a quieting are heard more often now, and not only from pastors and Sunday school teachers. Urgent warnings are coming from people working in technology and mental health. Just as the Church tells us to periodically limit or abstain from certain food, experts in these secular fields are saying that, for our own good, we need to seriously curtail or, in some cases, entirely eliminate the time we spend using smartphones, checking social media, and consuming news.

One such voice belongs to Jean M. Twenge, a psychologist whose research tracks changes in behavior and psychology between generations. She reports that starting "around 2012, I started seeing large, abrupt shifts in teens' behavior and emotional states."[43] Dr. Twenge had flagged important mental health markers,

---

42 *Great Lent*, 101.

43 Jean M. Twenge, PhD, *iGen: Why Today's Super-Connected Kids Are Growing Up Less Rebellious, More Tolerant, Less Happy —and Completely Unprepared for Adulthood—and What That Means for the Rest of Us* (New York: Atria Books, 2017), 4.

including depression, loneliness, anxiety, and suicide. She continues, "As I dug into the data a pattern emerged: many of the large changes began around 2011 or 2012. . . . Exactly when the majority of Americans started to own cell phones that could access the Internet, popularly known as smartphones."[44] The great risk, she found, was the instant connection to social media that smartphones provided to young people.

Another voice belongs to Georgetown computer science professor, Cal Newport. In *Digital Minimalism: Choosing a Focused Life in a Noisy World*,[45] Dr. Newport laments that our social, political, and economic world is now largely driven by an "attention economy" designed to steal our time and hijack our attention. Since much of the Internet is monetized by the number of clicks a website receives or the amount of time a visitor spends there, more clicks and more time equal more money. Content producers and social media influencers are incentivized to produce clickbait in which anything goes. Newport urges a simple cure: quit all optional social media immediately.

Finally, as innumerable critics and observers have stated, the news has become another form of

---

44   Ibid.
45   New York: Penguin Random House (2019).

entertainment, and the industry is in a steep and likely irreversible ethical decline. Any pretense to an unbiased, thoroughly investigated presentation of facts has been abandoned. Now news outlets mostly offer a limited menu of partisan propaganda, one-sided "discussions" of social issues, and unedifying celebrity gossip. News appeals to emotion rather than reason, fills us with anxiety, dehumanizes people who disagree, and distracts us from the real work God has set before us. Orthodox writer Nassim Nicholas Taleb suggests, "To be completely cured of newspapers, spend a year reading the previous week's newspapers."[46]

So life-pervading and addicting has digital technology become that asceticism in this area will require heroic levels of self-denial from many of us. Writing when there were only television and radio to contend with, Fr. Schmemann suggests as a "first custom" that

the use of TV and radio be drastically reduced during Lent. We do not dare to hope here for a "total" fast but only an "ascetical" one which, as we know, means first of all a change

---

46   Nassim Nicholas Taleb, *The Bed of Procrustes: Philosophical and Practical Aphorisms* (New York: Random House, 2015), 19.

of diet and its reduction. . . . What must be stopped during Lent is the 'addiction' to TV—the transformation of man into a vegetable in an armchair, glued to the screen and passively accepting anything coming from it.[47]

The principle still applies. Asceticism in this area means that at certain times of the day, on certain days of the week, and during certain weeks of the year, we consciously restrict how long and how often we're on our devices. This asceticism will foster an awareness of what we are doing online and why we went there. That awareness can restore to us the power to use our tools in a limited, purposeful, and controlled way. If Dr. Newport's recommendation to quit all social media seems too severe, we should at least stay away from it during Lent and on Wednesdays and Fridays.

There's more we can do. We can "dumb down" our smartphones by deleting unnecessary apps. We should restrict the times we spend on our phones and tablets or in front of a screen. From time to time, we should go on a news fast so we can ascertain how much our news consumption really improves our quality of life. Using our devices should be forbidden during prayer, at the dinner table, and when having a

---

47   *Great Lent*, 101–102.

conversation. For at least an hour before we go to bed and an hour after waking up, our devices should be strictly off limits.

Father Schmemann wisely tells us that "the silence created by the absence of the world's noises made available by the media of mass communication is to be filled with positive content."[48] A partial list of that positive content must surely include

- ✠ Prayer
- ✠ Having meaningful conversations
- ✠ Reading—for enjoyment as well as profit
- ✠ Actually listening to music rather than having it playing in the background
- ✠ Walking
- ✠ Taking a nap
- ✠ Simply sitting quietly.[49]

Establishing "environmental silence," as we are about to see, can lead to repentance.

---

48 Ibid.
49 One of Fr. Thomas Hopko's "55 Maxims for the Spiritual Life" echoes philosopher and mathematician Blaise Paschal's observation that "all of humanity's problems stem from man's inability to sit quietly in a room alone," which is often quoted in discussions about this topic.

9

Exorcise Your Mind

Once we establish a measure of environmental silence, something important happens: we become aware of our thoughts. We discover we can mark what we're thinking as impartial observers. Psychologists, instructors in Eastern meditation, and Christian teachers of prayer all remind us that we are not our thoughts. There is within us a faculty that stands apart from what is going on in our heads and allows us to identify and, when necessary, exert control over what we allow ourselves to think or imagine.

This is important because our struggle against sin is fought on three fronts: our words, our deeds, and our thoughts. Our minds are a battleground, and our enemy is scheming and fighting to dominate them.

C. S. Lewis's Screwtape recalls, "I once had a patient, a sound atheist, who used to read in the British Museum. One day, as he sat reading, I saw a train of thought in his mind beginning to go the wrong way. The Enemy, of course, was at his elbow in a moment. Before I knew where I was I saw my twenty years' work beginning to totter. . . . I struck instantly at the part of the man I had best under my control."[50] Screwtape introduced the thought that it was time for lunch, and ends by observing that "he is now safe in Our Father's house."

The work of discerning our thoughts marks the point where asceticism and repentance meet. In the original Greek of the New Testament, the word for repentance is *metanoia*. Literally, it means a "change of mind." To repent means to change not only how we behave, but also how we think and what we think. To embrace metanoia means to change our habitual ways of thought. It is "bringing every thought into captivity to the obedience of Christ" (2 Cor. 10:5).

If we read what the Fathers wrote about the ascetic life, we quickly realize that the task and technique of noticing and evaluating thoughts is a major concern. One collection of the sayings of the Desert Fathers

---

50   *Screwtape*, 2.

records over forty-five sayings about the matter.[51] The ascetic discipline of the early monks included the daily confession of their thoughts (not just their sins) to an older, more experienced monk. This provided an opportunity for the elders to instruct novices in the craft of recognizing and categorizing different species of thoughts.

The practice of guarding one's thoughts was often called "keeping vigil." In *The Arena*, St. Ignatius Brianchaninov describes it as "a firm control of the mind and posting it at the door of the heart, so that it sees marauding thoughts as they come, hears what they say, and knows what these robbers are doing, and what images are being projected and set up by demons, so as to seduce the mind by fantasy."[52] In *The Orthodox Way*, Archbishop Kallistos Ware compares the "discernment of thoughts" to our sense of taste: "spiritual taste, if developed through ascetic effort and prayer, enables a man to distinguish between various thoughts and impulses within him. He learns the difference between the evil and the good, the superfluous and the meaningful."[53]

---

51 Ward, *Sayings of the Desert Fathers*.
52 *Arena*, 129.
53 Kallistos Ware, *The Orthodox Way* (Crestwood, NY: St. Vladimir's Seminary Press, 1979), 115.

All of this is biblically rooted. For example, in Deuteronomy, Moses warns the Israelites to "Beware lest there be a hidden thought in your heart, a transgression of the law" (15:9). In Matthew, Jesus reminds His hearers that "out of the heart proceed evil thoughts, murders, adulteries, fornications, thefts, false witness, blasphemies" (15:19).

In prehistoric cultures, healers learned to distinguish poisonous plants from those that could heal. Similarly, to facilitate the work of discerning thoughts, monks compiled a list of the poisonous ones. These eventually became what is known in the West as the infamous seven deadly sins, better known among Orthodox as the passions.

The list of toxic thoughts/deadly sins includes vainglory, anger, lust, greed, gluttony, envy, and acedia (or sloth). Eastern writers include an eighth sin: pride. In the appendix of this book, you will find a brief field guide to this traditional list. It attempts to translate them into language that may be more readily recognizable for us today.

In *Acedia and Me*, an in-depth exploration of what may be the least understood of the major passions, Kathleen Norris writes, "What the church later defined as sin, desert monks termed 'bad thoughts' which to my mind is a much more helpful designation."[54] She bolsters this idea from her readings of the *Institutes* and *Conferences* of St. John Cassian. I'm inclined to agree. The list of passions works better when used for preemptive action rather than as an after-the-fact confessional catalogue.

The list provides a lexicon for naming our "bad thoughts" once we've noticed them. Naming something is powerful. To know the name of something is to hold a measure of control over it. If at a church convention I called out "Father!" fifty men in cassocks would turn around. If I called out "Father Andrew," the likelihood of my spotting the right priest would increase significantly. This is the reason Adam was first tasked with naming the animals in Eden and the reason Jesus, when He exorcised the Gadarene demoniac, began by asking its name (Gen. 2:19; Mark 5:9).

Left unrecognized or unchallenged, these toxic thoughts easily lead us into sin. However, if through prayer, fasting, and especially silence, we've learned to notice what we are thinking and which direction our stream of thought is flowing, we can name our thoughts. We can divert their flow. We can reject

---

54   Kathleen Norris, *Acedia and Me* (New York: Riverhead Books, 2008), 30.

them outright; we can "refuse the evil and choose the good" (Is. 7:16 NKJV).

Some Practical Thoughts

Many of our toxic thoughts come when we look at (or remember) our neighbor carnally or mercilessly. We stop seeing other people as human beings like us: created in God's image, redeemed by our Lord, and destined to be deified by the Holy Spirit. Our passionate thoughts strip away their humanity. Anger reduces them to something they did or said. Envy reduces them to their possessions or status. Lust reduces them to their bodies and the use we could make of them. Vainglory only values our neighbor as an admiring and appreciative audience. Acedia renders us dull and indifferent to God, neighbor, and creation alike—and even to ourselves.

The immediate question facing us is: Once we've noticed the toxic nature of these thoughts, how do we exorcise them?

1. FIRST, WE NAME THEM. If (more likely, when) you're driving and someone cuts you off and forces you to slam on your brakes so that your coffee spills all over, and the impulse to utter the usual words or make the customary gesture comes to

mind, call the thought by its name: "Anger." Say it out loud if you are alone. A gap will immediately open between stimulus and response, and in that narrow space, you can now choose your response. This is a skill; as with all skills, it improves with persistence and practice.

2. WE CAN DELIBERATELY SUBSTITUTE OTHER THOUGHTS IN THEIR PLACE. Prayer, of course, is always the best choice. Monastic writers have long recommended the Jesus Prayer or Psalm 69/70:1 ("O God, make haste to help me") for this purpose. A more specifically applicable verse comes from Psalm 50/51: "Create in me a clean heart, O God, / And renew a right spirit within me" (v. 12).

3. CHANGE THE SUBJECT. Think about something else: A problem at work. What's planned for supper tonight. Scheduling an oil change. The more innocuous and innocent, the better. After all, this is the tactic Screwtape employed with his patient in the British Museum, and two can play at that game.

4. DEPLOY ONE PASSION AGAINST ANOTHER. Our vanity is especially useful for this. If I lose my temper now . . . If I'm caught staring . . . If I keep bragging about this . . . What will other people think of me?

5. USE YOUR SENSE OF HUMOR OR IRONY. Again, we can be instructed by Screwtape's advice to his protege:

> Your patient has become humble; have you drawn his attention to the fact? . . . Catch him at the moment when he is really poor in spirit and smuggle into his mind the gratifying reflection, "By Jove! I'm being humble," and almost immediately pride—pride at his own humility—will appear. If he awakes to the danger and tries to smother this new form of pride, make him proud of his attempt—and so on, through as many stages as you please. But don't try this too long, for fear you awake his sense of humour and proportion, in which case he will merely laugh at you and go to bed.[55]

6. FINALLY, YOU HAVE THE POWER TO SIMPLY REBUKE THE THOUGHT. I have in mind something on the order of a stern "Get thee behind me, Satan!" but less dramatic or high-sounding: "Knock it off!" "Enough," or a disdainful "Oh, shut up" should be fine.

---

55 *Screwtape*, 69–70.

10

Be Purposeful

We return to our first question: Why do we fast? The Old Testament suggests fasting was practiced in ancient Mesopotamia for two reasons. First, fasting was an attempt to attract the gods' attention—a religious hunger strike, as it were. The Bible shows little regard for this kind of fasting. When the priests of Baal took things to extremes and "cried aloud, and cut themselves, as was their custom, with knives and lances, until the blood gushed out on them," the narrator simply remarks in one translation, "no one answered, no one paid attention" (1 Kings 18:28–29 NKJV). I'm sure the biblical author smirked as he wrote it.

Fasting also served to signal that people were

serious. After Jonah (finally!) delivered history's shortest sermon, the king hastily published a decree: "Let not the men, cattle, oxen, or sheep taste anything, eat, or drink water. . . . Who knows if God shall have a change of heart and turn from his fierce anger, that we should not perish?" (Jonah 3:7, 9). Supplementing prayer with fasting signaled that this was no casual request. The petitioners were willing to pay a steeper price to receive what they wanted.

All of which serves to remind us that fasting and its accessory ascetic practices are undertaken for purposes beyond themselves. They are a means, not an end, a path, not a destination. In helping us to prepare, to be free, and to be fruitful, they empower us to live out the purpose of our life. Charles Malik, the Lebanese philosopher and diplomat, expressed that purpose in these words: "To give [ourselves] to Christ and serve suffering humanity in His name and for His sake."[56]

In the Sermon on the Mount almsgiving is

---

56   Charles Malik, *The Wonder of Being* (Waco, TX: Word Books, 1974), 91. Charles Malik is one of Orthodoxy's unsung heroes of the twentieth century. As a philosopher, he studied under Alfred North Whitehead and Martin Heidegger. He was the UN ambassador from Lebanon and worked closely with Eleanor Roosevelt to draft the Universal Declaration of Human Rights.

mentioned before prayer and fasting.[57] However, these three practices are usually listed in a different order: prayer, fasting, and almsgiving. This may be because Christians understand that fasting is a pivot point. Fasting lifts our eyes to heaven, and so we pray. Fasting lowers our eyes to earth, and so we give.

Thus we fast because we are loved, and we fast to be better able to love.

---

57 Perhaps because almsgiving is the most public of the three practices and therefore the easiest one to show off.

A Field Guide to Toxic Thoughts

The List:

- ✠ Pride
- ✠ Vainglory
- ✠ Anger
- ✠ Lust
- ✠ Envy
- ✠ Greed
- ✠ Gluttony
- ✠ Acedia

Pride and Vainglory

Labeling pride a sin sounds strange. Is it wrong to take satisfaction in a job well done? Could it be a sin to feel proud when my child makes the honor roll, hits a home run, or graduates with honors? How can so natural a human feeling be called the mother of all vices and the root of all other sins? A different word is needed. I suggest "narcissism."

This term, originating in Greek mythology, now designates a psychological malady—the narcissistic personality disorder that politicians sometimes diagnose in their opponents. Since, as many have pointed out, the ascetic Fathers were psychologists before psychology was invented, the term is apt. From the theological point of view, narcissism is idolatry of self. Saint Benedict of Nursia tells us to "prefer nothing whatever to Christ,"[58] but because of narcissism we do the opposite: we prefer nothing more than our own self. To help us escape from the gravitational pull of the self and break free from the incessant orbiting around our desires, whims, and impulses, the Church gives us the gift of asceticism.

In the West, pride has been lumped together with something called "vainglory." The word has largely vanished from use (which is not surprising, since much of what we see in the media, marketing, and politics is precisely aimed at arousing this passion). Originally, the word "vain" described some useless

---

58   Benedict, *Rule*, 95.

and unprofitable activity. The best-known instance in the Bible is Qoheleth's repeated lament in Ecclesiastes, "Vanity, vanity, all is vanity." Applied to a person, the word is a synonym for "conceited" and the antonym of "modest."[59] It is not a widely admired personality trait. When Carly Simon sang, "You're so vain," she was not being complimentary. Vainglory, too, could benefit from a more easily understandable translation. I suggest "ego."

When St. Ignatius Brianchaninov discusses ego, he calls it "seeking [our] own glory and not God's,"[60] and later notes that "by its very nature, earthly and human glory is directly opposed to the glory of God."[61] He is echoing and expanding on Jesus' words in the Sermon on the Plain: "Woe to you when all men speak well of you, / For so did their fathers to the false prophets" (Luke 6:26).

Ego is not just being overly concerned about what others say about us behind our backs, how many followers we have on social media, or how many "likes" our latest tweet received. It is also about the things we secretly tell ourselves about ourselves. During quiet or

---

59   Modesty, while a desirable social trait, should not be mistaken for humility, a spiritual virtue.

60   *Arena*, 52.

61   *Arena*, 152.

boring stretches, our ego projects scenarios in which our witticisms garner admiration and our arguments skewer and silence our opponents. Whenever our ego is running rampant, we are in the grip of vainglory.

Anger and Lust

Here we face our two most deeply rooted and primal passions. They are biologically grounded and hard-wired into our bodies and brains. One is triggered by desire, the other by the frustration of desire. The animal part of our nature—what St. Paul calls the "flesh," the Fathers call our "carnal nature," and neurologists call our "mammalian brain"—compels us to focus on survival and reproduction. At issue is not just individual survival, but the survival of the group, be it herd, pack, or tribe. Lust serves to ensure the group will survive for future generations. Anger energizes us to protect our territory in order to ensure access to food and protect our offspring.

This is a good place to recall that the Fathers teach that the passions are all given to us by God, were meant to be used for good, and have been perverted as a result of the Fall. Anger was intended to fuel us to confront what is wrong about ourselves and our world and make it better. Greed and gluttony try to pervert the selfless, grateful delight we could otherwise take in God's good creation. Envy is the distortion of a desire to grow by becoming more like those we admire: it redirects our gaze from what they are to what they have. Lust perverts the desire to be united with those we love.

As Screwtape complains, "[God] has filled His world full of pleasures. There are things for humans to do all day long without His minding in the least—sleeping, washing, eating, drinking, making love, playing, praying, working. Everything has to be twisted before it's any use to us. . . . Nothing is naturally on our side."[62]

To my knowledge, no surveys have been taken nor are statistics available, but I suspect that sins born from anger and lust make up the bulk of the sins a priest hears in confession. As we age, their grip on us begins to loosen. This is one reason why, thankfully, some of us become wiser and kinder as we grow older. Nevertheless, the Fathers warn that the struggle with these two will last our lifetime.

Greed, Gluttony, and Envy

These three are closely related. For one thing, they are so much a part of our social/cultural environment,

---

62 *Screwtape*, 119–20.

they have merged so deeply into the background, that they easily go unnoticed. But like the others, they are constantly being used to steal our attention and drive our choices. In our homes and on the streets, greed, gluttony, and envy scream for our attention from TVs and billboards. Political ads (I'm writing this in an election year) are filled with thinly veiled appeals to greed or envy. It's no wonder that farmer and essayist Wendell Berry has indicted America as "a nation whose economy is founded foursquare on the seven deadly sins."[63]

Greed, gluttony, and envy reject limitations and constraints. In our minds, they whisper to us the same insistent and insatiable demand for *more*. They were forged and fully formed in Eden, where everything was given to Adam and Eve. Everything was theirs for the taking with only one restriction.

Our never-satisfied addiction to more is not limited to food and other material things. We are greedy for attention and envy the famous. We are greedy for novelty and envy others' experiences. We try to crowd and cram more and more into our day, forgetting the psalm verse we hear at every Presanctified Liturgy: "*It*

---

63   Wendell Berry, *Sex, Economy, Freedom & Community* (New York: Pantheon, 1993), 85.

is vain for you to rise up early, / To sit up late, / To eat the bread of sorrows; / *For so* He gives His beloved sleep" (Ps. 126/127:2 NKJV). Today there is even an acronym for it: FOMO—the fear of missing out.

Perhaps most destructive to our souls is the fact that greed, gluttony, and envy are inherently anti-eucharistic. They blind us to the embarrassingly obvious fact that everything we say is "ours" is ours as a gift, not as a right. Furthermore, what has been given to us was meant to be given through us to our neighbor. Every liturgy reengages us with this reality. Thus, we read in the opening pages of Fr. Alexander Schmemann's classic treatise on the sacraments, *For the Life of the World*, "the only natural (and not 'supernatural') reaction of man to whom God gave this blessed and sanctified world, is to bless God in return, to thank Him, and . . . in this act of gratitude and adoration—to know and possess the world."[64]

Acedia

Like pride, acedia is another of the seven bad thoughts that is usually misunderstood. It is sometimes translated "sloth" or "laziness." This may not

---

64 Alexander Schmemann, *For the Life of the World* (Crestwood, NY: St. Vladimir's Seminary Press, 1973), 15.

be inaccurate, but it is inadequate. Inactivity is the obvious visible symptom of acedia, but the underlying condition is harder to define.

The English language has had recourse to slow-moving examples from the animal kingdom: the slug and the sloth. Some one hundred Bible verses describe sloth and chastise the slothful. It is no surprise we find many of these verses in Proverbs. Yet sloth still eludes a clear definition.

Using via negativa, it may help to distinguish acedia from other forms of inactivity.

To rest is not to surrender to acedia. Nor is acedia to be mistaken for leisure. Noting that our word "school" comes from the Greek word for "leisure," philosopher Josef Pieper exalts leisure as "the basis of culture"[65] because it gives us time for pursuits that go beyond mere survival.

Following the practice of early Fathers and modern psychologists, listing the diagnostic signs or symptoms of acedia may be more helpful. Acedia is perhaps best characterized by the refusal to take interest in anything outside ourselves. It is the passion characterized by a lack of passion.

---

65   This is the title of Pieper's classic book on the topic (San Francisco: Ignatius Press, 1952).

Acedia shows itself in the unwillingness to assume responsibility, to take action, or to make and honor commitments. An entire industry has arisen to exploit, indulge, and perpetuate our acedia. It encourages us to live vicariously through celebrities and watch talk shows rather than engage in conversation. The most obvious—and dangerous—symptom of acedia is passivity.

About the Author

L. Joseph Letendre is the author of the popular guide *Preparing for Confession* and the companion to this volume, *When You Pray: A Practical Guide to an Orthodox Life of Prayer* (Ancient Faith Publishing, 2017). His writing has also appeared in *Touchstone, The Reformation and Revival Journal,* and *St. Vladimir's Theological Quarterly.* He recorded the audiobook of St. Nicholai Velimirovic's *Prayers by the Lake* for Ancient Faith Publishing. He holds degrees in psychology, philosophy, and education, as well as an MDiv from St. Vladimir's Seminary. He is a parishioner at All Saints Antiochian Orthodox Church in Chicago, Illinois.